EASY CELEBRATION CAKES

For Abel

EASY CELEBRATION CAKES

Fun ideas for all occasions

SIMON &
SCHUSTER

London · New York · Sydney · Toronto · New Delhi

A CBS COMPANY

First published in Great Britain as *Cakes For Fun*
by Simon & Schuster UK Ltd, 2005
A CBS Company

This edition published exclusively for Poundland Ltd
by Simon & Schuster UK Ltd, 2014

Simon & Schuster UK Ltd
222 Gray's Inn Road
London WC1X 8HB
www.simonandschuster.co.uk

Simon & Schuster Australia, Sydney
Simon & Schuster India, New Delhi

10 9 8 7 6 5 4 3 2

Design: Pauline Hull
Photography: Juliet Piddington
Styling: Helen Trent
Photograph on page 6: Andres Poveda, courtesy of Poundland

Printed and bound in China

ISBN 978-1-4711-4068-6

Contents

Introduction

For a special occasion there's nothing quite like a home-made cake in the centre of the table and my baking range available in Poundland means it needn't be expensive to bake at home. What would a birthday or anniversary be without the wishing, cutting and blowing out of candles that's become such an important part of the ritual of celebration? For most of us, though, hours of mixing, icing, piping and moulding are out of the question: life's on the whole too short and too busy to spend days producing something that's going to be destroyed and eaten in a matter of minutes.

It doesn't mean, though, that your cakes have to be boring. There are many ways of producing beautiful decorations without having to be technically proficient at all – using ready-made icing, for instance, is exactly like rolling out play dough – and all the ideas in this book are extremely easy to do, enormous fun to look at and delicious to eat. I've given the quantities in terms of my Poundland packet mixes and ready-made icings as well as recipes from scratch, so it's up to you how much you do yourself.

Many of the ideas are interchangeable for different occasions, people and age groups, and I've included loads of cup cakes: these are wonderfully adaptable and useful for anything from weddings to school functions. I'm sure you'll be inspired to experiment and improvise: once you've mastered the basic techniques you'll be able to create all kinds of different designs, and if you want to incorporate a particular character, it's simple to add a plastic Noddy, Mr Incredible, Batman or whoever to cakes like the Dinosaurs, Butterflies & Flowers or Train. They could even be sitting on cup cakes or popping out of parcels – only you know what'll thrill the guest of honour (nothing would do for my youngest on his second birthday but a vacuum cleaner cake – unfortunately, at thirty, he no longer shows any sign of his early obsession).

Finally, it's worth remembering that, for children in particular, too much sugar too often is not a good idea. I'm sometimes asked if I have any 'slimming' cake recipes: as a cake is essentially a delicious concoction of sugar, butter, eggs and flour this has always seemed to me a bit of a contradiction in terms, but I do think that cakes, especially ones like these with all the icing involved, should be kept for the occasional tea and for special celebrations. They'll be all the more appreciated.

Jane

Recipes

Cake mix and icing

I have based every cake idea in the book on standard quantities of cake mix and icing. You can use my Poundland cake mixes (vanilla, chocolate or lemon sponge and cookie mix) following the quantity guidance below, or make the cakes entirely from scratch using the recipes here. You'll need to make the gingerbread, fridge cake and brownie mixes yourself, but they're very simple and excellent for children to do (particularly the fridge cake, as it doesn't need baking).

1 quantity of sponge mix =
1 packet of my Jane Asher Poundland cake mix (vanilla, chocolate or lemon) or
1 quantity of all-in-one sponge recipe

1 quantity of brownie mix =
1 quantity brownie recipe

1 quantity of vanilla cookie dough =
2 packets of my Jane Asher Poundland cookie mix or 1 quantity vanilla cookie dough recipe

1 quantity of royal icing =
1 quantity of royal icing recipe

1 quantity of chocolate fudge icing =
2 tubs of my Jane Asher Poundland chocolate frosting or 1 quantity of chocolate fudge icing recipe

1 quantity of American frosting =
2 tubs of my Jane Asher Poundland white frosting

Cake recipes – *all give 1 quantity*

1 quantity all-in-one sponge cake
125 g (4½ oz) soft butter or margarine   2 medium eggs
125 g (4½ oz) caster sugar   1 level teaspoon baking powder
125 g (4½ oz) self-raising flour, sifted   (omit baking powder for cup cakes)

Preheat the oven to Gas Mark 4/180°C (fan oven 160°C)/350°F (the sponge is cooked at the same temperature for all cake shapes). Grease and flour the tins. Line the base of the larger tins with baking parchment as well. Put all the ingredients into a bowl or food processor and mix with a wooden spoon

– or process on high speed – for about 2 minutes, or until smooth. Pour the mixture into the prepared tin and refer to the cooking times below. All the cakes are cooked when firm to touch or the blade of a knife inserted into the centre comes out clean.

Adding flavours (per quantity)

For vanilla sponge add 1 teaspoon vanilla essence.
For chocolate sponge replace 25 g (1 oz) flour with 25 g (1 oz) cocoa powder.
For coffee sponge add 2 tablespoons of instant coffee dissolved in 2 tablespoons of boiling water.
For lemon or orange sponge add the grated rind of 1 lemon or orange and a squeeze of juice.

1 quantity all-in-one sponge makes:	cooking time:
2 x 18 cm (7 in) round sandwich tins	20–25 minutes
36 mini cup cakes	10–12 minutes
18–20 regular cup cakes	12–15 minutes
15 cm (6 in) square deep cake tin	1–1¼ hours
15 cm (6 in) round deep cake tin	1–1¼ hours

2 quantities all-in-one sponge makes:	cooking time:
1 large tiffin tin	1¼–1½ hours
1 large spherical cake tin (baked in two halves)	50–60 minutes
20 cm (8 in) square deep cake tin	1–1¼ hours
20 cm (8 in) round deep cake tin	1–1¼ hours

3 quantities all-in-one sponge makes:	cooking time:
25 cm (10 in) round deep tin	1¼–1½ hours
25 cm (10 in) square cake tin	1¼–1½ hours

1 quantity chocolate fridge cake

350 g (12 oz) chocolate
125 g (4½ oz) butter
2 tablespoons golden syrup
450 g (1 lb) cake crumbs

4 tablespoons brandy (optional)
225 g (8 oz) crushed digestive biscuits
50 g (2 oz) glacé cherries

Put the chocolate, butter and golden syrup into a heatproof bowl over a pan of simmering water, stirring occasionally until the mixture is melted together (or melt in the microwave). Remove from the heat and stir in all the other ingredients. Transfer into the container and chill until set.

Chocolate brownie

75 g (2¾ oz) dark chocolate (50–70%
   cocoa solids), in chips or roughly chopped
150 g (5½ oz) butter
300 g (10½ oz) caster sugar
3 medium eggs
150 g (5½ oz) plain flour
450 g (1 lb) dark chocolate buttons with
   50–70% cocoa solids

Preheat the oven to Gas Mark 6/200°C (fan oven 180°C)/400°F. Grease a baking tin and line the base with baking parchment. Melt the chocolate and the butter together, either in the microwave or in a bowl over a pan of simmering water. Add the sugar, eggs and flour to the chocolate and mix well. Stir in three-quarters of the chocolate buttons. Pour into the lined baking tray and sprinkle on the remaining chocolate buttons.

Cook for roughly 30–40 minutes (depending how gooey you like them) or until firm to the touch. Allow to cool in the tin.

One quantity fills:

30 x 20 x 2.5 cm (12 x 8 x 1 in) deep tray-bake tin
23 x 7 cm (9 x 2¾ in) heart-shaped cake tin

Vanilla cookie dough

280 g (10 oz) plain flour
200 g (7 oz) firm butter
100 g (3½ oz) icing sugar
2 egg yolks
1 teaspoon vanilla extract or essence

Preheat the oven to Gas Mark 6/200°C (fan oven 180°C)/400°F. Grease two baking trays or line with baking parchment. Put the flour in a bowl. Cut the butter into small pieces and add to the flour. Rub the butter into the flour with your fingertips until the mix looks like breadcrumbs.

Add the sugar, egg yolks and vanilla extract or essence and mix to a dough. Put into a plastic bag and chill for at least 30 minutes. Roll out the dough on a lightly floured surface and cut out as required. Bake for about 8–10 minutes or until golden brown around the edges. Leave to cool and harden on a wire rack.

Gingerbread

350 g (12 oz) plain flour
2 teaspoons baking powder
2 teaspoons ground ginger
110 g (4 oz) firm butter
175 g (6 oz) light muscovado sugar
3 tablespoons golden syrup
1 egg

Preheat oven to Gas Mark 6/200°C (fan oven 180°C)/400°F. Grease two baking trays or line with baking parchment. Put the flour, baking powder and ginger into a bowl. Cut the butter into small pieces and add to the flour mix. Rub the butter into the flour mix with your fingertips until the mixture looks like breadcrumbs. Add the sugar, syrup and egg and mix to form a dough. Put into a plastic bag and chill for at least 30 minutes. Roll out the dough on a lightly floured surface, cut out as required and bake for about 12 minutes or until golden brown around the edges. Leave to cool and harden on a wire rack.

Icing recipes – *all give 1 quantity*

Butter cream

100 g (3½ oz) butter, softened
½ tablespoon milk
150 g (5½ oz) icing sugar, sifted

Put the butter into a bowl with the milk and mix together well. Beat in the sifted icing sugar a little at a time, until the mixture is light and creamy. Store in an airtight container in the fridge until needed. Bring to room temperature before using.

Adding flavours (per quantity)

For vanilla butter cream add 1 teaspoon vanilla extract or essence.
For lemon butter cream substitute 1 tablespoon lemon juice for the milk.
For chocolate butter cream add 150 g (5½ oz) melted dark chocolate.
For coffee butter cream add 2 tablespoons instant coffee dissolved in a little hot water. Omit the milk.

Chocolate fudge icing

280 g (9¾ oz) caster sugar
80 g (3 oz) butter
100 g (3½ oz) dark chocolate
  (50–70% cocoa solids), in chips or
  roughly chopped

140 ml (4½ fl oz) milk
A pinch of salt
2 teaspoons vanilla extract or essence

Mix all the ingredients except the vanilla extract or essence in a saucepan. Heat it to a rolling boil, stirring occasionally. Boil for 1 minute without stirring. Now place the saucepan in a bowl of iced water and beat continually until the frosting becomes a smooth, spreadable paste. Lastly, stir in the vanilla essence.

Royal icing

1 egg white
250 g (9 oz) icing sugar, sifted

Put the egg white in a bowl and beat lightly with a fork to break it up. Beat in the icing sugar a little at a time until the icing is firm and glossy. For coating consistency, add a little water.

Chocolate ganache

450 g (1 lb) dark chocolate (50–70% cocoa solids), in chips or roughly chopped
300 ml (10 fl oz) double cream

Put the chocolate in a heatproof bowl. Heat the cream gently in a saucepan until boiling, and then remove from the heat and pour it over the chocolate. Stir until the chocolate has melted and blended with the cream into a rich, dark mixture. Allow to cool a little, but use while it is still of a pouring consistency.

Techniques

All the techniques used in the book are pretty simple. Just think of roll-out icing as the equivalent of pastry, or even play dough, and food colours as paints.

Shaping and trimming the cake

There is very little shaping of the cakes in this book, but for splitting and trimming it really helps to use a long, sharp, serrated knife.

Filling and covering a cake with butter cream and roll-out icing

To start, cut the cake in half horizontally and sandwich it back together with butter cream. Having done that, spread a little butter cream or jam over the top and sides of the cake. Put it into the fridge for 30 minutes to chill and firm up, which will make it far easier to cover with icing. Knead the icing until it is soft and then, using a rolling pin, roll it out to roughly the right size on a surface lightly dusted with icing sugar. Roll the paste up on to the pin to lift it and unroll it again over the cake. Gently smooth the paste over and around the shape of the cake. Trim any excess from the bottom edges of the cake with a sharp knife.

To colour roll-out icing

You can buy many different ready-coloured icings from my shop, but when you need to make your own simply add a little food colour and knead well until the colour is evenly mixed in. For making really pale, pastel colours liquid food colours will work, but for any deeper colours you'll need to use paste food colours, or the icing will get far too sticky. Colour marzipan in the same way.

Painting with food colours

Use either liquid or paste colours, but, again, for strong, bright effects you'll need the paste ones. Simply paint them on to dry icing with an ordinary paintbrush. For large areas or to make lighter colours, dilute them with a little water; for stronger effects use them neat.

Adding names and inscriptions to cakes

There are various easy ways of personalising cakes. You can pipe wording with ready-to-use gels or icings, buy some chocolate or icing letters and numbers, write with food colour pens or paint with food colours (either freehand or with stencils). For special occasions you can buy, by mail order from my shop, edible printed plaques to attach to the cake.

Adding candles

I've shown all the cakes without candles, but you'll want to add some to birthday cakes. There are all kinds of candles and holders available, and it's easy to push them into the cake. If you're worried about spoiling the design, stick the candles on to the cake board instead. Do this by shaping some tiny pieces of roll-out icing into balls, stick them to the board with a little water and push the candles into them.

Icing the cake board

I've only covered the boards with icing in a couple of the recipes, but it does finish off a cake beautifully if you can be bothered. Stick the cake to the board with a little butter cream or icing. Dampen the rest of the board with a little water, roll out some icing in a strip and trim one long side straight. Stick it to the board, putting the straight edge up against the bottom edge of the cake – do this in two or three sections if necessary, then trim neatly around the outside edge. Another way is to simply spread the board with royal icing and swirl it roughly with a palette knife (very good for water or snow effects!).

Adding dowels to layered cakes

This is done to help the lower cakes support the upper ones in designs like the Love Heart or Chocolate Wedding cakes, and is extremely simple to do. Make three, four or five little marks (as required in the recipe) with a pin or tip of the knife on the icing of the largest cake, spacing them evenly and within the circumference of the tier above. Push the plastic dowels gently into the cake and make a mark on them, level with the top of the icing. Take them out and cut with a sharp knife or pliers, then put them back into the cake, checking that they are flush with the surface. Do this for each tier except the top one.

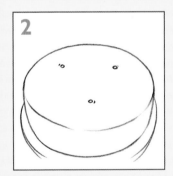

Making white, gold or silver stars and hearts

To make about 15 large stars or hearts: roll out 50 g (1¾ oz) white icing to about 5 mm (¼ in) thick, and, for a gold or silver finish, brush the icing with gold or silver dusting powder, using a dry paintbrush. Cut out hearts or stars with shaped cutters. You can also buy these ready-made, on or off wires.

For wired stars and hearts

As above, then dip the ends of a wire in water and push into each heart or star while still soft. Wires can be cut to different lengths as necessary. Let them dry overnight.

Equipment & Ingredients

*None of the equipment or ingredients – the tins, boards, icings, mixes, glues, sprinkles, colours etc – that I've used in the book is hard to get hold of. Some can be found in supermarkets, or everything is available from our London shop, either in person or online at **www.janeasher.com**; **info@janeasher.com** (Tel: 020 7584 6177).*

Equipment

With the following equipment you can produce any or every cake in this book, but not all of it is essential. With a little improvising, you can make do with what you have – occasionally, though, it's worth investing in the real thing.

Cake tins

Most of these cakes can be made if you have just a few standard cake tins: you'll find some excellent non-stick ones in my Poundland range or by mail order from my shop. If you choose non-stick, then you don't have to line the sides, although it's worth putting non-stick baking parchment or greaseproof paper in the bottom.

To make the cakes in this book you'll need:

23 cm (9 in) heart cake tin – or you could use a 25 cm (10 in) square tin and cut the heart shape out of it, but you'll obviously have some cake left over (use in trifles or fridge cakes).

1 large tiffin tin (see page 17) – this makes the Pink Princess' skirt (p 64). You could use a pudding basin, but the proportions are not as good and you'll find you use the tin for other ideas once you've got it.

1 large spherical tin – for the Christmas Pudding (p 22), the Witches' Cauldron (p 52), Penguin Snowball (p 18) and Page 3 (p 36). Two pudding basins can be used instead, but they'll need a lot of trimming. The sphere is brilliant for other cake ideas such as footballs and globes, not to mention for making old-fashioned round steamed Christmas puds.

1 large and 1 small egg mould – for the Easter Bunny on page 50. You could use the packaging around Easter eggs instead.

1 x 13 cm (5 in) flowerpot – for the Flowerpot on page 48.

Plus:

2 x 18 cm (7 in) round sandwich tins

20 cm (8 in) round loose-bottomed tin

15 cm (6 in), 20 cm (8 in) and 25 cm (10 in) round deep tins

15 cm (6 in) and 25 cm (10 in) square deep tins

30 x 20 cm (12 x 8 in) by 2.5 cm (1 in) deep tray-bake tin

1 bun tray

1 muffin tin

1 mini muffin tin

30 x 20 cm (12 x 8 in) baking tray

Other equipment

Cake boards – many of the cakes can be put on plates, but for a 'professional' finish there's no doubt boards are the thing, and they're very inexpensive. For some of the designs (such as the wedding cakes) they're essential. 'Drums' are the thicker type that are used most of the time; the thinner ones (usually sold as 4 mm) are needed for layered cakes such as the Love Heart Wedding cake or for when you don't want the board to show. If I don't specify which type then it really doesn't matter which you use.

Mini and regular paper cup cake cases – these come in all kinds of exciting designs these days, including gold and silver, so don't feel you have to stick to the old-fashioned white ones.

Rolling pin – for rolling out the icing, which is the simplest way of smoothly covering a cake.

Ribbed rolling pin – this is for the Box of Roses on page 40. It's not essential but you'll love the effect.

Side smoother – this is a small plastic gadget a bit like the tool masons use for cement when building a wall. It makes it very easy to get a good smooth finish after covering a cake with roll-out icing, and I recommend investing in one.

Assorted cookie cutters – plastic or metal.

A large serrated knife – great for carving, slicing and trimming the cakes when necessary.

Palette knife – not essential, but it does make it easier to apply butter cream and other icings.

Small, sharp knife – well, I assume you've got one anyway, unless you're strictly a baked beans and takeaway person, but then I don't suppose you'd be using this book.

Piping bags and nozzles – these are not needed for most of the cakes (and don't be put off by the mere sound of them). No complicated piping is called for, but it's a good thing to have one on standby for the odd occasion. If you don't fancy making your own out of paper, then an ordinary plastic one with an adaptor plus a no. I and a shell nozzle should cover everything. If you use the ready-made decorating icings and writing icings then you won't have to bother, as they come with the nozzles all in.

Christmas tree cutters (see below) – for the Christmas Cookie Tree on page 24. You can either use a ready-made set of cutters from my Poundland range or cut cardboard shapes from the template on page 24.

Blossom cutters – these are tiny cutters with plungers that make it very easy to cut out little flowers. If you don't want to bother, then ready-made icing flowers or even pretty little sweets can always be substituted.

Food colour pens – if you don't feel happy writing or decorating with a paintbrush and food colour, then these can be useful. They're just like felt tip pens, but filled with edible colour.

Paintbrushes – absolutely no need for anything specialised. An ordinary small brush will do nicely, to be used for painting with food colours and for sticking things with edible glue.

Posy picks – it's not considered a good thing to stick flowers and leaves straight into cakes these days (I hate to think of all the plant poison my family and I must have eaten before the health and hygiene laws got going), and these clever little plastic gadgets are like miniature vases. You just push the pointed end into the cake and then arrange the flowers, wired stars or whatever into the top, filling in any gaps with icing to keep the flowers in place. Very inexpensive and a great buy.

Doll pick – this is the modern version of the 'crinoline lady' that you push into the top of a cake 'skirt' to make it look like a doll, fairy etc. For children, I think it's more fun to use a doll, wrapping the legs in cling film or even, if necessary, removing the legs altogether (but do make sure they're replaceable, or there'll be tears before bedtime…).

Food grade wires – again, we are governed by health laws nowadays, and if you need wires in a cake (as with the gold stars, bats and hearts in this book) then you need to use 12-gauge covered wires. It's a very easy, showy way of adding height and drama to cakes and puds, and worth having a packet in the cupboard.

Dowels – these are used when you're piling up layers, as for wedding cakes. Nowadays they are plastic, and extremely easy to use, as shown in the techniques on page 13.

Cup cake stands – these can be hired from specialist cake suppliers or you can buy pretty cardboard ones.

Ingredients

Cake and cookie mix

See the recipe section for details of the different types of cake I've used in the book. You may even be able to find some cakes ready-made that are the right sizes. I've used sponge cake for most of these designs, which can be any flavour you fancy, although I've stuck to chocolate, vanilla and lemon. This can either be home-made or from cake mixes (I've given you the necessary quantities in the recipe section). There are also some designs using chocolate fridge cake mix, which is great for children to use, as it involves no baking.

Icings

Roll-out icing – I've tended to use this to cover most of the cakes, simply because it's so easy to use and achieves such a good finish, but, obviously, if you're a dab hand with royal icing then that's just as good in most instances, although when any kind of modelling is called for then the roll-out is essential. You can buy it in loads of different colours from my shop, and you'll always find white (and a small selection of colours) in supermarkets. If you can't find the colour you want then it's very easy to colour your own.

Butter cream – can be either bought ready-made in tubs, or home-made.

Royal icing – not necessary in all the cakes, but good for piping and flooding the tops of cup cakes. Again, this can be bought ready-made, or you can use a mix (Nigella's favourite for her cup cakes!) or home-made.

Decorating icing, writing icing, gels etc – you can now buy brilliant tubes of ready-made icing in packs with nozzles all ready to go. The smaller tubes of writing icing are great for adding names and greetings, and the gels come in handy for extra decoration. There are even glittery edible gels now, which are amazing (see the Pink Princess, page 64).

Food colours – these are available as liquids or pastes. For all painting effects and for adding to butter cream or royal icing liquid ones work well, although as they'll make the texture more runny you need to add them drop by drop while the icing is still stiff. Because of this, they're not as good as paste for kneading into roll-out icing, which, except for pastel colours, they tend to make too sticky.

Gold dusting powder – dusting powder gives a beautiful burnished finish when added to icing with a dry paintbrush, and they come in all kinds of wonderful colours. I've used gold on the stars for the Christmas parcel (p 26), for instance.

Edible gold leaf – occasionally I've used a little gold leaf, which, lifted on with a dry brush, gives a very glamorous finish. It comes in pots or packets of 1 sheet or more.

Sparkles and sprinkles – when you want a really glittery effect (and, being showbiz myself, I frequently do!), as in the Penguin Snowball or the Smartie Wedding and on the cup cakes, you need to use 'iridescent sparkle', which comes in all sorts of beautiful colours. Sprinkles can be bought in every shape, size and colour.

Sweets and strands – I found most of the ones I've used in supermarkets, but it obviously depends on the time of year for certain shapes. You won't find many bats and pumpkins in the spring, for example, or Father Christmases in the summer. Keep an eye out, too, in newsagents: they often have great shapes in their pic 'n' mix, or in assortment bags.

Edible glue – sounds a bit of a contradiction in terms, but it does exist. Used just like real glue, and very handy for sticking on bits of decoration.

Edible hearts and stars – these are available ready-made in white, gold or silver and either attached to wires or on their own. You can easily make them yourself (see Techniques, page 13).

Edible photographs, pictures and labels – as used in Healthy Eating on page 38 and the decorated cup cakes. This is modern technology put to an unexpected use! Any photograph, piece of text, painting etc can be sent to my shop (www.janeasher.com), either electronically or in the post, and we'll send you an edible version in food colour on a frosting sheet. This can be peeled off its backing sheet and stuck to the icing.

Penguin Snowball

This reminds me of snow scenes on the Christmas cakes of my childhood. My mother would pull the bright white icing into peaks just as I have here, and then add a plaster Father Christmas, a couple of wiry fir trees and a Yule log topped with a robin that was almost as big as Santa. The thought of those cakes still brings back the almost unbearable excitement of the approaching big day.

I spherical sponge cake
(see pages 8–9)

I quantity butter cream
(see page 11)

500 g (1 lb 2 oz) white
roll-out icing

I quantity royal icing
(see page 11)

250 g (9 oz) black roll-out
icing

Orange food colour

White iridescent sparkles or
edible glitter

20 cm (8 in) round cake
board

1 Split each half of the sphere horizontally and sandwich together again with one third of the butter cream. Stick the two layered halves together with another third of the butter cream.

2 Spread the remaining butter cream in a thin layer all over the sphere, then chill for 30 minutes to firm up. Roll out 400 g (14 oz) white icing and cover the cake, smoothing the icing around the sphere with your hands. Trim as necessary. Keep the trimmings to one side.

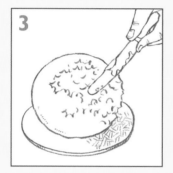

Put the cake on the cake board. Spread the royal icing all over the cake and pull into peaks with a blunt knife or fork.

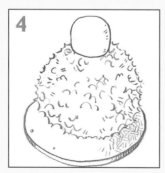

Roll 125 g (4¹/₂ oz) black icing into a ball and stick on top of the cake to make the head.

5 Make two small balls from the white icing trimmings and, with a little water, stick them on for eyes. Then add two smaller black balls for the pupils. Divide the remaining black icing in two and roll into balls. Flatten each into a wing shape and push into the white icing.

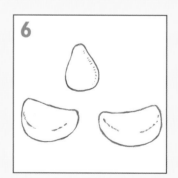

Colour the remaining white icing orange. To make the beak, roll about half the orange icing into a ball and taper it at one end to form a cone shape. Flatten the wider end and stick to the face with a little royal icing.

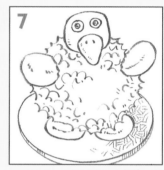

Mark on the mouth and nostrils with the back of a small knife. Roll the remaining orange icing into a ball, flatten and cut in half for the feet. Stick to the base of the cake. Lastly, dust the cake with iridescent sparkles.

Snowman

This is exactly the same principle as the Baby on page 70 and this shape can also be used to make various animals if you like. This snowman would look very good on a snowy background, which you could easily add by spreading some royal icing on the board, pulling it into peaks with a knife and then sprinkling on some edible sparkle.

1 quantity sponge mix baked in 2 x 18 cm (7 in) round sandwich tins (see page 8)

1 quantity butter cream (see page 11)

800 g (1 lb 11 oz) white roll-out icing

150 g (5½ oz) brown roll-out icing

50 g (1½ oz) black roll-out icing

75 g (2¾ oz) red roll-out icing

Orange food colour

Sweets

46 x 30 cm (18 x 12 in) cake board

1 Put both the cakes on the cake board and spread them with the butter cream.

2 Roll out a third of the white icing and cover one of the cakes, trimming away the excess (reserve the trimmings for later). Repeat with the other cake, and then push them both together.

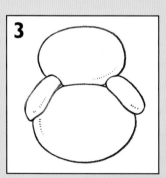

3

Roll out the remaining white icing into a sausage about 25 cm (10 in) long, and cut it in half to make the arms. Stick the arms to the sides of the lower cake with a little water.

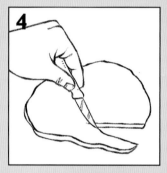

4

For the hat, roll out half of the brown icing, then trim one edge straight with a sharp knife. Stick this to the top of the head with the straight edge across his forehead using a little water. Trim the icing around the head.

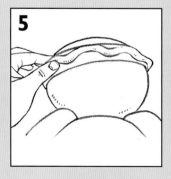

5

Roll the remaining brown icing into a long sausage about 23 cm (9 in) long. Flatten it slightly and stick to the base of the hat to form the rim.

6

With the black icing, make two small balls for the eyes and three larger ones for buttons. Stick on to the cake. Add a very thin sausage of black icing for the mouth, adding two small balls of white icing (from the trimmings) for cheeks.

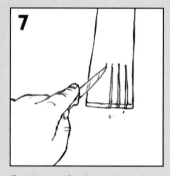

7

For the scarf, roll out the red icing thinly and cut into three strips. With the back of a small knife, mark tassels on the ends of two strips and stick them to the cake. Stick the third strip round the neck.

8 Colour the remaining white icing orange and make a cone shaped nose and stick in place.

9 Decorate the hat with small colourful sweets or any leftover icing.

Christmas Pudding

I first made this design many years ago and it's still one of my favourites. I've given two versions here. The first is a very speedy one using ready-made chocolate icing and paper holly, and the second — for real chocoholics — is covered with a chocolate ganache and decorated with edible holly.

Simple version

1 spherical chocolate sponge cake (see pages 8–9)

1 quantity butter cream (see page 11)

500 g (1 lb 2 oz) chocolate-flavoured roll-out icing

50 g (1¾ oz) raisins

150 g (5½ oz) white roll-out icing

Ready-made holly sprig

20 cm (8 in) round board

Richer version

As for simple version, but without the ready-made holly sprig, plus:

Extra 50 g (2 oz) white roll-out icing

1 quantity chocolate ganache (see page 11)

Yellow, green and red food colours

Holly cutter

For the simple version

1 Slice each half of the sphere in two horizontally, then sandwich together again with one third of the butter cream. Stick the two layered halves together with another third of the butter cream. Spread the remaining butter cream all over the cake in a thin layer. Chill for 30 minutes to firm it up.

2 Roll out the chocolate icing and drape it over the cake, smoothing with your hands and trimming the excess from around the bottom as necessary.

3 Put the cake on the cake board and stick the raisins on with a little water. Roll out the white icing and cut a rough shape for the cream. Stick to the top of the cake with a little water and add the holly sprig.

For the richer version

Follow up to the end of Step 2 of the method for the simpler version. Put the cake on to a cooling rack with a sheet of greaseproof paper underneath. Pour over the chocolate ganache, making sure that the cake is completely coated.

Let it cool a little and, once the ganache is sticky, add the raisins.

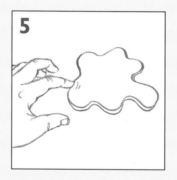

Colour 150 g (5½ oz) of the white icing pale yellow. Roll it out and cut a rough shape for the cream. Stick it to the top of the pudding and smooth down the edges.

Colour approximately 30 g (1¼ oz) of the white icing green, roll out and cut out three holly leaves. Stick to the top using a little water. Colour the remaining icing red and roll into five small balls for the berries. Stick them on with a little water.

Christmas Cookie Tree

This remarkably effective and beautiful Christmas tree is simply a stack of cleverly cut gingerbread cookies with some added icing. It makes a wonderful alternative for the table for those who don't like Christmas cake – and you could always use a cookie mix recipe instead of gingerbread, if you prefer. You can either buy the set of 10 cutters from my shop (see page 15 for details), or make cardboard templates from the patterns on this page and cut around them into the dough.

- 2 quantities of gingerbread dough (see page 10)
- 2 quantities of royal icing, coating consistency (see page 11)
- 1 quantity royal icing, for piping
- Green food colour
- 25 g pot of 8 mm silver balls or dragees
- 1 pot of chocolate beans
- 1 pot of white iridescent sparkles or edible glitter
- 1 cookie tree cutter set or card templates made from the patterns on this page
- Piping bag with adaptor and no. 3 nozzle

1 Preheat the oven to Gas Mark 6/200°C (fan oven 180°C)/400°F. Grease two baking trays or line them with baking parchment.

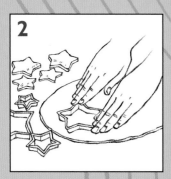

Roll out the gingerbread on a surface lightly dusted with flour. Cut out two of each size star cutter as directed in the set, or cut round two of each size of the card templates. Place them on the prepared trays and bake for about 12 minutes or until golden brown around the edges. Leave to cool. You'll have to do this in batches, as there'll be 20 cookies.

3 Colour the coating consistency royal icing green, and then pour or brush it over the top and sides of all the cookies. Allow to dry for about 1 hour.

4 Assemble the tree by sticking each layer, using more royal icing, to the top of the previous one. Make sure that the points of the star shapes are placed alternately as shown in the picture. Stick the top star upright.

5

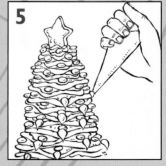

Pipe icing on to the corners of the cookies and let it drip over the edges. Stick the silver balls and chocolate beans on to the icing. Lastly, sprinkle all over with the white sparkles.

Parcels For All Occasions

A wrapped present brings with it a sense of promise and excitement. You'll find that once you've mastered this, a cake parcel is a really effective way of making a centrepiece for a variety of occasions. I've given you four ideas here, but there's no end to the different ways of decorating them – little individual cake parcels at each place setting could look stunning at a party.

For each parcel, split the cake in half and sandwich together with three-quarters of the butter cream. Place the cake on the board. Spread the remaining butter cream in a thin layer over the top and sides. Chill to firm. Cover with roll-out icing and trim the base, keeping the trimmings as necessary. Mark 'paper' folds on two sides with the back of a knife.

Valentine parcel

1 Cut two strips of ribbon long enough to go over the sides and top of the cake and stick them on with a little edible glue. Stick on the silver hearts and then a bow, made from the remaining ribbon.

Christening parcel

1 Add the ribbon as for Valentine parcel.

2 Divide the trimmings of the white icing into three. Using the food colours, colour each piece differently. Roll out the pieces thinly and cut out various shapes with the cutters. Stick the shapes on with the edible glue.

Christmas parcel

1 Use the icing trimmed from covering the cake to make the gold stars, unless bought ready made. Roll out the red icing into an oblong 35 x 15 cm (14 x 6 in). Cut two long strips 35 x 2.5 cm (14 x 1 in) and stick them both ways across the cake to make the ribbon, trimming the ends to fit snugly at the base. Cut out two more strips 10 x 2.5 cm (4 x 1 in) and trim one end of each at an angle.

2 Stick both strips to the centre of the 'ribbon' to make the ends of the bow. Cut a strip 30 x 5 cm (12 x 2 in). Dampen the centre of the strip, fold each end into the middle and squeeze together to make the bow. Turn it over, then cut out and stick on a thin strip for the knot. Using the back of a small knife mark on fold lines around the knot. Stick the bow on to the cake with a little water.

3 Stick on gold stars with a little water. Insert the posy pick into the cake at the back of the bow and stick in the stars on wires using a little icing to keep them in position.

Birthday parcel

1 Using the food colours mixed with a little water, paint on balloons and streamers. Leave for a couple of hours to dry. Follow the Christmas parcel method for the ribbon and bow.

For each parcel

15 cm (6 in) square sponge cake (see pages 8–9)

1 quantity butter cream (see page 11)

20 cm (8 in) square cake board

Valentine parcel

500 g (1 lb 2 oz) red roll-out icing

1 metre (1 yard) silver ribbon

Edible glue

14 mini silver chocolate hearts

Christening parcel

500 g (1 lb 2 oz) white roll-out icing

1 metre (1 yard) yellow ribbon

Blue, yellow and green food colours

Cutters – toys or animals etc

Edible glue

Christmas parcel

500 g (1 lb 2 oz) white roll-out icing

200 g (7 oz) red roll-out icing

5 gold stars (see pages 13, 17)

1 packet gold stars on wires (see pages 13, 17)

1 small posy pick (see page 16)

Birthday parcel

500 g (1 lb 2 oz) white roll-out icing

200 g (7 oz) red roll-out icing

Blue, yellow and red food colours

Fine paintbrush

chocolate Gâteau

Beautiful chocolate cakes don't come much simpler than this. Some of the ready-made decorations around now look really stunning, and the hours you would have had to spend piping delicate chocolate leaves can be used instead for something really important ... like reading Hello or watching EastEnders.

2 x 18 cm (7 in) sandwich sponge cakes (see pages 8–9)

1 quantity chocolate butter cream (see page 11)

1 quantity chocolate ganache (see page 11 – don't panic, it's really easy)

1 box chocolate leaves or shapes

¾ metre (30 in) gold ribbon

1 sheet edible gold leaf (optional)

23 cm (9 in) round cake board or plate

1 Place one of the sponges, flat side down, on the cake board or plate. Spread the top liberally with a layer of chocolate butter cream. Place the other cake on top, bottom side up so that you have a flat surface. Press the cake down until it is level.

2 Cover the sides with more butter cream, smoothing with a palette knife and filling in any holes. Chill to firm.

3 Place the cake on a cooling rack over a sheet of baking parchment to catch drips. Pour the ganache over, making sure the cake is coated. Allow to set.

4 Using a palette knife, lift the cake back on to the board or plate. Arrange the chocolate leaves and shapes around the top. Finish with the ribbon and, if you like, lift pieces of gold leaf on to it with a dry brush.

Decorated Cookies

I've used the American term for these because I love US cookie recipes and decoration ideas and it sounds somehow cosier and less formal than our 'biscuits'. They're great for any time of year – even just as a treat for tea – but work particularly well at Christmas, when you can make them spicy and comforting for nibbling yourself or offering to guests with a mug of hot chocolate or glass of mulled wine.

1 quantity gingerbread or vanilla cookie dough (see page 10)

2 quantities royal icing (see page 11)

Food colours

Tubes of writing icings and gels

Selection of sprinkles, sparkles, sweets, ready-made decorations etc

Cookie cutters

1 Preheat the oven to Gas Mark 6/200°C (fan oven 180°C)/400°F. Grease two baking trays or line with baking parchment.

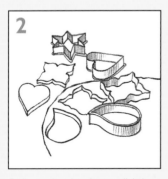

2 Roll out the dough on a lightly floured surface and cut out different shapes. Bake for about 12 minutes until golden brown around the edges. The cookies will still be soft, but will harden as they cool. Remove from the oven and allow to cool for a few minutes, before transferring to a rack to cool completely.

3 Colour the royal icing in batches, not letting it get too runny (see page 17) and spread over the cookies.

4 Alternatively, you can 'flood' them. To do this pipe a little line around the edge of each cookie with writing icing, then

add some water to the royal icing to make it runny. With a spoon, gently fill the piped outline with the runny icing letting it flood to the edges.

5 Add sprinkles, ready-made decorations or sweets and pipe on some extra details.

To make Christmas tree decorations

Poke a hole in the top of each cookie with a straw or skewer before cooking. Once cool and decorated, add a pretty ribbon for hanging on the tree.

Rainbow Balloons

This is another idea using cup cakes, but this time with mini cakes covered in gorgeously coloured sprinkles. You can buy these or make your own (see below). These little cakes are extremely pretty and can be used in all kinds of different designs – they look fabulous arranged as a rainbow (see page 1) just piled up on a pretty plate.

You can't get much simpler than this. I pinched the idea from an American magazine, and it's a wonderfully easy way to give a celebratory feel to a party table. I have to admit, though, it does look best viewed from directly above, as in our photograph… consider inviting only extremely tall people to your celebration.

Rainbow

1 quantity sponge mix (see page 8)

1 quantity butter cream (see page 11)

1 pot each of red, yellow, pink, lilac sprinkles

10 edible gold stars (see pages 13 and 17)

1 pot of white iridescent sparkles or edible glitter

About 40 mini cup cake cases

Mini muffin baking tin

35 cm (14 in) square cake board or tray

1 Preheat the oven to Gas Mark 4/180°C (fan oven 160°C)/350°F. Put the cup cake cases into the muffin tin and, with a spoon, half-fill with the cake mixture. Bake for about 8–10 minutes until firm to the touch or golden brown. Allow to cool on a rack. If the cakes have domed during cooking trim the tops so they are flat and below the level of the paper cases.

2 Using a palette knife, spread a thin layer of butter cream on each cake. Put some sprinkles on a saucer and dip each cup cake in, pressing lightly so that the top is fully coated. Repeat with all the colours leaving 10 cakes plain. Finish the plain ones with an edible gold star and white iridescent sparkles.

3 Arrange the rainbow on the cake board or tray.

To make your own sprinkles

Place 25 g (1 oz) granulated sugar into a plastic bag and add a tiny amount of food colour. Shake well until all the sugar is coloured.

Balloons

1 quantity sponge mix (see page 8)

1 quantity butter cream or royal icing, coating consistency (see page 11)

Blue, red, green and yellow food colours

18–20 paper cup cake cases

4 metres (4 yards) of 4 mm wide ribbon – 1 metre of each colour to match the icing

Bun or muffin tin

20 x 40 cm (8 x 16 in) cake board

1 Preheat the oven to Gas Mark 4/180°C (fan oven 160°C)/350°F. Put the cup cake cases into a bun or muffin tin and, with a spoon, half-fill the cases with the sponge mix. Bake for about 10–15 minutes until they are firm to the touch and golden brown. Remove the cakes from the tin and allow to cool completely on a rack. If they have domed during cooking, trim off the tops so they are flat and below the level of the cases.

2 Divide the icing into four bowls and colour with the food colours. Spoon the royal icing over the cup cakes and then allow it to set, or spread with butter cream.

3 Cut the ribbons into strips and arrange them on the board, with the ends tucked under the cakes.

Chocolate Cascade

Almost everyone loves chocolate, and it's really easy to make a spectacular 'gâteau' without any piping or fancy icing simply by decorating with chocolate and sweets. You can go for a classy look using only elegant, delicate chocolates and silver or gold almonds or you can turn it into something much more brash and jolly using Smarties and brightly coloured sweets.

2 x 18 cm (7 in) round chocolate sponge cakes (see pages 8–9)

1 quantity chocolate butter cream (see page 11)

1 quantity chocolate fudge icing (see page 11)

Selection of sweets and chocolates

23 cm (9 in) round cake board or plate

1 Put one of the cakes flat side down on the plate or cake board, spread with a generous layer of chocolate butter cream and put the other cake on top – bottom side up so that you have a flat surface.

2 Press down until level, then spread the top and sides with the remaining butter cream and smooth with a palette knife, filling any holes. Chill for about 30–60 minutes to firm.

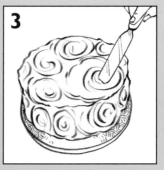

Cover the top and sides with the fudge icing and, using the edge of the palette knife, make swirls all over the top and sides.

4 Decorate with your favourite sweets and chocolates, bringing them right down the side to cascade on to the board, sticking with a little fudge icing as needed.

Page 3

These would make great cakes for a stag night — wonderfully politically incorrect and terrific fun. If you don't have a spherical tin, then you could bake them in two heatproof pudding basins — but they'd end up a bit too voluptuous for most tastes.

1 spherical sponge cake (see pages 8–9)

1 quantity butter cream (see page 11)

400 g (14 oz) pale pink roll-out icing

2 glacé cherries

30 x 20 cm (12 x 8 in) cake board

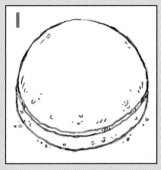

Slice each half of the sphere in two horizontally and sandwich them back together with butter cream.

2 Spread a thin layer of butter cream all over each dome, reserving a small amount. Chill to firm.

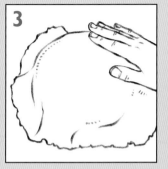

Roll out half of the icing into a circle about 30 cm (12 in) across to cover one dome, trimming away the excess with a sharp knife. Repeat for the other.

4 Place the cakes on the cake board and stick a cherry on to the centre of each with a tiny bit of butter cream.

Healthy Eating

In my second ever cake book I made something very like this and called it Diet Cake – but today's obsession with health foods and ingredient lists has inspired me to rename it and make it more gloriously gluttonous than ever. You can send off for the edible printed label (see page 17), or write on a piece of clean card and remove it before eating. Enjoy!

Nutritional Information

Carbohydrates ... excessive

Fat .... ludicrous

Sugar .... over the top

Salt .. unnecessary amount

Vitamins .... minimal

Omega 3 .... non-existent

Protein .... trace

Calories ....

don't even ask

2 x 18 cm (7 in) round sponge cakes (see pages 8–9)

1½ quantities of butter cream (see page 11)

Cream cakes, e.g. éclairs, biscuits, sweets, chocolates or whatever you fancy

1 aerosol tin of double cream

Edible printed label (see page 17 or make a label with card)

Tape measure (make sure it is clean)

25 cm (10 in) round cake board or plate

1 Put one sponge cake flat side down on to the board or plate. Spread generously with about a third of the butter cream.

2 Place the other cake on top, domed side up. Press it down gently so the butter cream oozes out a little.

3 Spread the top with the remaining butter cream.

4 Pile up the cakes, biscuits, chocolates, sweets and so on as lavishly as possible, sticking them together and filling in any gaps with the squirty cream (this bit's enormous fun).

5 Add the printed ingredients label. Finally, stick the tape measure around the cake with a little more cream.

Nutritional Information

Carbohydrates.... excessive
Fat............. ludicrous
Sugar........ over the top
Salt.... unnecessary amount
Vitamins....... minimal
Omega 3.... non-existent
Protein..... trace

Calories...

don't even ask

Chocolates & Roses

A box design is very easy and can be filled with all kinds of different things. The box of chocolates can be as elegant or as much fun as you want, filling it with bright sweeties or sophisticated marrons glacés.

The box of roses is a stunning variation and a design I used in tiers for my stepdaughter's wedding cake. You could make it without the ribbed sides, but it adds a fantastic texture and sets off the flowers beautifully.

Box of chocolates

15 cm (6 in) round sponge cake (see pages 8–9)

1 quantity butter cream (see page 11)

750 g (1 lb 10 oz) roll-out cream or white icing

18 chocolates

Edible glue

18 petits fours cases

20 gold stars (see page 13)

1.5 metres (1½ yards) gold ribbon

20 cm (8 in) round cake board

1 Slice the cake in two horizontally and sandwich together with about a third of the butter cream. Put the cake on the board. Spread the rest of the butter cream all over the top and sides. Chill to firm.

2 Roll out 220 g (7½ oz) of the icing. Cut out a 15 cm (6 in) round disc and place it on top of the cake.

3 Roll out the remaining icing into a long strip about 48 x 9 cm (19 x 3½ in). Trim one long edge straight. Dampen the edge of the icing with a little water.

4 Roll up the strip on the rolling pin and then unroll again on to the side of the cake, straight edge down, pressing gently into place. Trim the join, then trim the top edge straight, allowing about 1 cm (½ in) to stand above the level of the cake.

5 Put the chocolates into the petits fours cases and stick to the top of the cake with a little edible glue.

6 Stick the stars to the side of the cake with edible glue (you can use flat sweets or jellies instead) and finish by adding a ribbon bow with two long ends stuck under the base of the cake with a little edible glue.

Box of roses

15 cm (6 in) round chocolate sponge cake (see pages 8–9)

1 quantity butter cream (see page 11)

750 g (1 lb 10 oz) chocolate roll-out icing

Ribbed rolling pin (optional)

19 cm (7½ in) diameter disc of cellophane or clingfilm

8 large fresh roses (approx)

Bear grass (buy this from florists or use any greenery)

Half a small Oasis sphere, soaked in water

20 cm (8 in) round cake board

1 Split the cake in half horizontally and sandwich together with about a third of the butter cream. Put on the board. Spread the rest of the butter cream over the top and sides of the cake. Chill to firm.

2 Roll out 220 g (7½ oz) of the icing and cut a 15 cm (6 in) disc and place on top of the cake. Moisten the edge of the icing with a little water.

3 Roll out the remaining icing into a long strip about 48 x 9 cm (19 x 3½ in). Now roll along its length with the ribbed pin and then trim one edge straight. Roll the strip up on to the pin and unroll again on the side of the cake, with the straight edge to the bottom.

4 Trim the join and stick the ends neatly in place using a little water. Trim the top edge straight, allowing about 1 cm (½ in) to stand above the level of the cake.

5 Put the disc of cellophane into the top. Arrange the roses and grass in the Oasis and place on top of the clingfilm or cellophane.

Snake & Caterpillar

This is a good way to use cup cakes, and if you can't find exactly the same sweets as I've used here, there are plenty of others that look suitably serpentine. I warn you, though, that there may be a fight over who gets the head: you could consider a many-headed snake – a kind of hydra of the tea table.

The delight of this kind of design is that it can be made to feed any number of people and requires no cake tin – or cutting. This caterpillar is only to give you inspiration as he could be decorated in a manner of ways to great effect. Putting the legs and boots in place will either give you hours of fun or drive you nuts.

Snake

- 1 quantity sponge mix (see page 8), depending on length of snake needed
- 1 quantity butter cream (see page 11)
- Yellow food colour
- 3–4 rainbow drops (chocolate buttons topped with sprinkles) per cup cake
- 1 pot of jelly diamonds
- 2 Smarties
- 1 liquorice lace
- 1 pot of green sprinkles
- 18–20 cup cake cases
- Bun or muffin tray

1 Preheat the oven to Gas Mark 4/180°C (fan oven 160°C)/350°F. Arrange the cup cake cases in a bun or muffin tray and spoon in the mixture. Bake the cup cakes for about 10–15 minutes. Repeat as necessary. Allow to cool and then trim flat the tops of any that have domed during cooking.

2 Colour the butter cream yellow. Using a small palette knife, spread the icing on top of each cake, reserving a little.

3 Put two or three rainbow drops down the centre of each cup cake. Using a little butter cream, stick a jelly diamond on top of each.

4 Arrange the snake on a tray, cake board or even along the centre of the table, on a paper tablecloth. Now add the Smarties for eyes and the liquorice lace for the tongue. Sprinkle the snake all over with green sprinkles.

Caterpillar

- 1 quantity sponge mix (see page 8)
- 1 quantity butter cream (see page 11)
- Green food colour
- Smarties
- 75 g (2¾ oz) mini chocolate buttons
- 1 packet red liquorice laces
- 1 packet thick red liquorice strands
- Black liquorice to make boots!
- 18–20 cup cake cases
- Bun or muffin tray
- Large cake board or tray

1 Preheat the oven to Gas Mark 4/180°C (fan oven 160°C)/350°F. Arrange the cup cake cases in a bun or muffin tray and spoon in the mixture. Bake the cup cakes for about 10–15 minutes. Repeat as necessary. Allow to cool and then trim flat the tops of any that have domed during cooking.

2 Colour the butter cream pale green and, with a small palette knife, spread the icing over the entire surface of each cake.

3 On all but one of the cakes, make a small V with mini chocolate buttons and place a Smartie in the middle. Arrange the cakes on a tray or board.

4 Cut the red liquorice laces into 1 cm (½ in) lengths and push them into the sides of the cup cakes. Cut the liquorice strands into 4 cm (1½ in) lengths and bend them into the sides of the cakes, placing a black liquorice boot at the end of each.

5 Decorate the remaining cup cake with two Smarties for eyes, a liquorice strand cut in half makes a nose and a big smile. You can use a matchmaker broken in two for the antennae (or use a red lace or strips of black liquorice).

Decorated Cup Cakes

Cup cakes have become very trendy over the last few years. They've metamorphosed from tea treats you'd bake with Mum on the kitchen table after school into a whole archipelago of beautiful, funny or stylish little cakes with personalities all of their own. They avoid the potential minefield of cutting a large cake, need no cake tins, boards (or even plates), can be stacked on different display stands according to the occasion and are quick and easy to make, decorate and eat. Generally good news all round.

1 quantity sponge mix (see page 8)

1 quantity royal icing, coating consistency, or butter cream (see page 11)

Decorations, sweets, food colours, edible pictures (see page 17), chocolates, piping tubes, gels etc

Iridescent sparkles or edible glitter – for an extra bit of magic

18–20 paper cup cake cases

Bun or muffin tin

Piping bag, adaptor and star or shell nozzle (optional)

1 Preheat the oven to Gas Mark 4/180°C (fan oven 160°C)/350°F. Put the cup cake cases in a bun or muffin tin and, with a spoon, half-fill the cases with the sponge mix. Bake for about 10–15 minutes until firm to the touch and golden brown. Remove from the tin and allow to cool completely on a rack. If the buns have domed during cooking, trim the tops so they are flat and below the level of the paper cases.

To ice with royal icing, simply spoon on to the top of the cake.

For butter cream, either simply spread over the top of the cake with the flat of a knife or pipe with a large nozzle in a swirl.

The instructions for these are to let your imagination run riot. Have a look at what we've done to some of the cakes in the photograph: you'll find they're really easy to copy and will inspire ideas of your own. Either pipe your own patterns or use entirely ready-made decorations – there are some terrific ones in the shops now. Let the children join in – some of the wittiest and most creative cake designs come from the youngest members of the family. There's nothing more satisfying than sitting round a table with cakes, icing and assorted decorations and letting everyone have a go. You could even use it as a game at a party – decorate your own cup cake for tea (if you can face the mess).

Chocolate Heart

You can't get much simpler than this, but the combination of chocolate and red hearts is irresistible. It is perfect for Valentine's Day – either at tea time or as a delicious pudding course in the evening, served with raspberries and some cream or crème fraîche. If you don't want to make the sparkly hearts, decorate the cake with red sweets instead.

23 cm (9 in) heart-shaped brownie (see page 10)

1 quantity chocolate fudge icing (see page 11)

100 g (3½ oz) red roll-out icing

1 pot of red iridescent sparkles or red edible glitter

1 pot of gold iridescent sparkles or edible glitter

Heart cutters in three sizes

28 cm (11 in) heart cake board (optional)

1 Place the brownie heart on the cake board or a pretty plate. Spread the fudge icing on the top, using a palette knife to make swirls.

2 Roll out the red icing and dampen with a little water; sprinkle with red iridescent sparkles or lustre sparkles and pat down gently. Using the heart cutters, cut out a selection of hearts and lay these on top of the cake.

3 Sprinkle the cake with gold iridescent sparkles or edible glitter.

Flowerpot

A tall cake makes a terrific centrepiece, but it's not easy to give height without resorting to tiers and the like, so I was very pleased with this idea.

I've given you two ways of finishing off the flowers, one slightly easier than the other. They both look great, I think.

1 quantity chocolate fridge cake (see page 9) to make 1 pot

½ quantity vanilla cookie dough (see page 10)

500 g (1 lb 2 oz) white roll-out icing

Food colours or some pretty sweets

1 x 100 g tub of milk chocolate honeycomb pieces

1 plastic flowerpot approx 12 cm (4½ in) diameter and 12 cm (4½ in) deep

Large flower cookie cutters

3 wooden kebab skewers

Fine paintbrush

20 cm (8 in) round cake board

To decorate the flowers

1 quantity royal icing (see page 11)

Food colours (green, orange, red, yellow)

No. 1 piping nozzle and piping bag **or** assorted sprinkles, hundreds and thousands, silver balls etc

1 Preheat the oven to Gas Mark 6/200°C (fan oven 180°C)/400°F. Line the flowerpot with clingfilm and fill with the fridge cake mixture. Chill for 2–3 hours.

Roll out the cookie dough to 5 mm (¼ in) thick. Cut out three large flowers with the cookie cutters. Cut out several more as spares or for party bags.

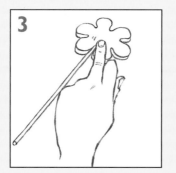

Press one end of a skewer into each flower and place on a greased or lined baking tray, making sure the biscuits and skewers are flat. Cut three leaves from the dough and add to the tray. Bake for 6–10 minutes. Allow them to cool on the tray.

4 Turn the cake out, removing the clingfilm, and put it on the cake board. Dampen the sides with water. Roll out the icing into a large oblong. Trim one edge straight, roll the icing back on to the pin and unroll it around the cake, straight edge

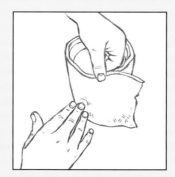

down. Trim the join and top, allowing about 2 cm (¾ in) to stand above the cake.

Paint around the top of the flowerpot using food colours mixed with a little water (or stick

on some sweets). Sprinkle the honeycomb on top for the soil.

6 To decorate the flowers: colour a quarter of the royal icing green, adding a little water, and paint the leaves with it. Divide the remaining icing into three and colour with red, orange and yellow, adding a little water. Put one colour into the piping bag. Pipe on petal outlines and flower centres. Add a little water to the remaining icings and, using the bag without a nozzle, fill in the outlines, using a contrasting colour for the centres. (Or spread the flowers with coloured icing and add sweets and sprinkles.) When dry, insert the skewers in the pot and add the leaves with a little icing.

Easter Bunny

If you're organised enough to keep the plastic mould from around an Easter egg until the following year, you can use it to make this cake. (Of course, you could buy the egg a little early and eat it quickly to free up the mould – it's a tough life, but someone's gotta do it.) Otherwise you'll need to buy proper egg moulds, which you'll be able to use over and over again to make your own chocolate Easter eggs if you get really keen.

1 quantity chocolate fridge cake (see page 9)

2 quantities of white American frosting or 2 quantities butter cream (see page 11)

11 pink mini marshmallows

2 pink Smarties

1 tube of brown writing icing

6 chocolate Matchmakers

1 large (18 cm/7 in long) and 1 small (10 cm/ 4 in long) Easter egg mould or packaging from Easter eggs

Large piping bag with adaptor and no. 8 star nozzle (optional)

30 x 25 cm (12 x 10 in) cake board

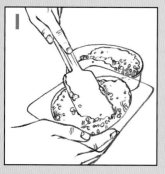

1 Divide the fridge cake between the two egg moulds and smooth the tops level. Put in the fridge for 1–2 hours or until firm.

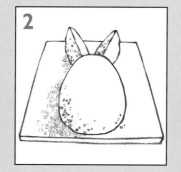

2 Turn the cakes out of the moulds and put the large one flat side down on the cake board. Cut the small egg in half lengthways, trim off about 1 cm (½ in) from the bottom of each piece, then place them at the top of the large cake to make ears. Tuck the trimmings under the ears to push them up.

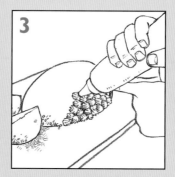

3 Put the frosting or butter cream into the piping bag fitted with a star nozzle and squeeze small stars all over the head and ears or swirl it on with a fork and pull up to make it furry.

4 Stick five mini marshmallows down the centre of each ear and use one for the bunny's nose. Stick on the Smarties for eyes and pipe the mouth on with the brown icing. Finish off by adding Matchmaker whiskers.

Witches' Cauldron

I hate to think how this spell is going to turn out – the local shops were fresh out of eye of newt or toe of frog, and could I find poisoned entrails anywhere? So I'm afraid it's all going to go horribly wrong. Never mind – these sugary snakes and worms will be appreciated for their taste, if not their magic properties, as a spooky treat at Halloween.

1 spherical sponge cake (see pages 8–9)

2 quantities chocolate butter cream (see page 11)

500 g (1 lb 2 oz) black roll-out icing

1 tube of green piping gel

An assortment of sweets, such as jelly bats, wriggly worms, sugary snakes and red jelly sweets

Food grade wire (see page 16)

3 chocolate flakes

1 pot of chocolate sprinkles

25 cm (10 in) round cake board

1 Split each half of the sphere in two and then stick them back together with butter cream. Sandwich the two layered halves together with more butter cream.

2 Trim off a small amount of sponge from the top and bottom of the sphere to flatten the surfaces. Put the cake on the board, then spread a thin layer of butter cream all over it (there will be some left over). Chill to firm.

3 Roll out the black icing and cover the cake, trimming off the excess around the bottom.

4 To make the rim of the cauldron, roll the trimmings into a long sausage and stick to the top, using a little water. Spread the leftover butter cream roughly on the cake board.

5 'Fill' the top of the cauldron with sweets and pipe on the green gel, allowing some to drip down the sides. To finish, add some jelly bats on wires. Cut some red jelly sweets into flames, and tuck them around the bottom of the cauldron with a few chocolate flake 'logs'. Add some chocolate sprinkles to the board.

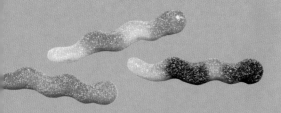

Dinosaurs

Ideas for boys can be tricky to come up with, but good old prehistoric monsters still seem to be holding their own against film and TV characters, computers, MP3 players, mobile phones and so on. Make them as scary or friendly as you see fit – a bit of added red piping gel round the mouths is good for flesh-eating dinosaurs and may please some of the more bloodthirsty partygoers. You can make the cookies a few days in advance if you keep them in an airtight container.

1 quantity gingerbread dough (see page 10)

2 quantities butter cream (see page 11)

Green, yellow, red, brown and orange food colour

1 x 20 cm (8 in) square sponge cake (see page 8)

1 quantity royal icing, coating consistency (see page 11)

1 pack of writing icing tubes

Selection of coloured sprinkles

Chocolate sprinkles

Dinosaur cookie cutters

Cocktail sticks

2 large baking trays (or cook in batches)

35 cm (14 in) square cake board

1 Preheat the oven to Gas Mark 6/200°C (fan oven 180°C)/400°F and lightly grease two baking trays.

2 Roll out the gingerbread dough on a lightly floured surface to about 5 mm (¼ in) thick. Cut out a selection of dinosaur shapes with the cutters. Re-roll the trimmings and cut out some grasses and rocks with a small sharp knife.

3 Put the gingerbread shapes on the baking trays and bake for about 12 minutes or until golden brown around the edges. Leave on the tray for a few minutes before transferring to a rack and leaving to cool completely.

4 Colour the butter cream green with the food colour. Put the cake on the board and spread the top and sides with the green icing, spiking up the top to look grassy. Spread a thin layer of butter cream on the board around the cake.

5 Divide the royal icing into four or five and mix with different food colours. Put the cookies on the rack over baking parchment to catch the drips. Pour a small amount of icing in the middle of each cookie and spread with the back of a teaspoon. Let the icing dry a little and, using the icing tubes, pipe on details, then add the coloured sprinkles. The rocks and grass can be decorated with any royal icing coloured green or with any remaining butter cream.

6 Arrange the cookies on the cake, adding cocktail sticks behind the dinosaurs for extra support if needed (but don't forget to take them out before eating!). Finally, add the chocolate sprinkles to the board.

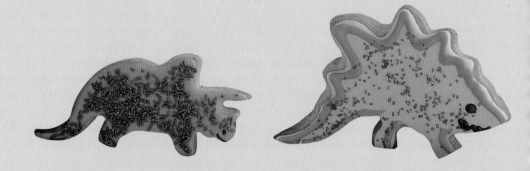

Football Shirt

The extraordinary appeal of football seems as strong as ever, and this simple design can be easily adapted to suit any team or school by changing the colours. You can either cut out the name and numbers freehand with a sharp knife, or invest in some cutters. You can, of course, adapt this design and use different coloured icing and decorations for an alternative T-shirt.

25 cm (10 in) square sponge cake (see pages 8–9)

2 quantities butter cream (see page 11)

1 kg (2 lb 4 oz) blue roll-out icing

150 g (5½ oz) white roll-out icing

Letter and number cutters (optional)

40 cm (16 in) square cake board

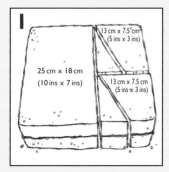

Trim the edges from the cake and slice the top flat. Cut the cake in two horizontally and sandwich together with half the butter cream. Then cut the cake as shown here. Keep the leftover pieces of cake for making trifles or fridge cake.

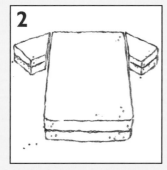

Place the large rectangle on the centre of the cake board. Using butter cream, stick the sleeve pieces to the large cake as shown. Spread the remaining butter cream in a thin layer over the whole cake. Chill to firm.

3 Roll out the blue icing and drape over the cake, smoothing with your hands and trimming as necessary. Mark the sleeve seams with the back of a knife.

4 Thinly roll out 100 g (3½ oz) of the white icing. Cut four strips 0.5 x 15 cm (¼ x 6 in). Attach the strips to the sleeves, using a little water. Trim the ends.

5 Thinly roll out a further 75 g (2¾ oz) of white icing and cut out a name and number. Stick on with a little water.

6 Roll the remaining white icing into a long sausage about 2 cm (¾ in) wide x 15 cm (6 in) long and stick to the top of the cake for the collar.

pizza

*I've always enjoyed the joke of one kind of food
looking like another, particularly when
it involves two totally different types of taste,
as in this savoury pizza reproduced
in sweet cake and icing.
For a larger party, simply use a whole quantity
of cake mix, either as a 'deep pan pizza'
in the 20 cm (8 in) tin or as
a 'thin and crispy' in a 25 cm (10 in) round tin.
Remember to use double quantities
of the other ingredients.*

½ quantity chocolate fridge cake
  (see page 9)

150 g (5½ oz) cream roll-out icing

3 tablespoons strawberry jam

A selection of sweets, e.g. dolly mixtures,
  jelly tots, chocolate beans

A small bar of white chocolate, grated, or a little
  desiccated coconut

20 cm (8 in) loose-bottomed round cake tin

25 cm (10 in) round cake board

1 Line the cake tin with
clingfilm, fill with the fridge
cake mix and smooth the top
with a knife. Chill for at least
2 hours.

2 Turn the cake out of the tin
and remove the clingfilm.
Put the cake on the cake board,
then dampen the surface of the
cake with water.

3 Roll out the icing and cover
the cake, trimming the base.
Spread over the strawberry jam
and add the sweets.

4 Sprinkle the white
chocolate or coconut
over the top.

Rocket & Train

Travel themes always go down well, and using Swiss rolls like this is an easy way to make all kinds of vehicles as the cakes come ready made. It may not be the most sophisticated of decorations, but the lively colours and bright sweets will make this very popular at birthday parties for younger children.

Rocket

1 Swiss roll

1 quantity butter cream (see page 11)

Yellow food colour

3 chocolate mini Swiss rolls

1 ice cream cone

3 marshmallows, cut in half

6 strawberry twists or ready made red piping gel

1 packet alphabet icing decorations

35 x 25 cm (14 x 10 in) cake board

1 Colour the butter cream yellow. Put the Swiss roll on the cake board and coat it with the butter cream. Then coat all three mini Swiss rolls and attach them to the base of the large Swiss roll.

2 Add the ice cream cone on the top, and then stick the marshmallow pieces on the mini rolls to make the rocket boosters.

3 Decorate the sides of the rocket boosters and ice cream cone with strips of strawberry twists or pipe on lines using ready-made red piping gel. Finally, give the rocket a name with alphabet icing decorations.

Train

25 cm (10 in) square sponge cake (see pages 8–9)

1 Swiss roll, 18 cm (7 in) long

2 quantities butter cream (see page 11)

Green food colour

8 round chocolate biscuits

6 strawberry twists, 1 packet liquorice allsorts, 2 liquorice pinwheels

1 tube of black writing icing

30 x 20 cm (12 x 8 in) cake board

1 Colour half the butter cream green. Cut the square sponge exactly in half vertically and round off one end to make the front of the train. Split both halves of the cake in two horizontally and sandwich together with the plain butter cream. Put one half on to the board.

2 Cut the remaining half of sponge in half, making two 13 cm (5 in) squares. Put the Swiss roll on the rounded sponge base towards the front, and add one of the small squares at the back. Trim down the height a little, and round the corners to make a curved roof.

3 Lastly, trim the remaining small square of sponge and put it at the back of the train for the coal fender.

4 Coat all of the train in the green butter cream. Stick four biscuits to each side of the train for the wheels. Put the strawberry twists across the engine as shown and finish with liquorice stripes and allsorts. Pipe on eyes and eyebrows with the writing icing.

Treasure Chest

There are some subjects that remain popular with children down the years for no apparent reason and, although pirates are more likely to be stealing intellectual property nowadays than doubloons and strings of pearls, a treasure chest remains a firm favourite for birthday cakes. This is also a useful technique for making boxes of chocolates, jewellery boxes and other less macho variations.

- 25 cm (10 in) square sponge cake (see pages 8–9)
- 2 quantities butter cream (see page 11)
- 1 kg (2 lb 4 oz) brown roll-out icing
- 400 g (14 oz) yellow roll-out icing
- 1 pot of edible glue
- 5 tablespoons brown sugar
- Chocolate gold coins
- Boiled sweets for jewels
- 25 g pot of edible pearls, silver balls or tiny mints
- 2 necklace sweets
- Cocktail stick
- 30 x 20 cm (12 x 8 in) cake board

1 Trim the crust and cut the sponge exactly in two vertically. Cut the top of one half into a slope, starting high at the front edge and going down by about 2.5 cm (1 in) at the back.

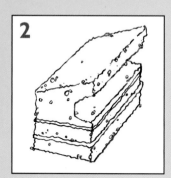

2

Cut a wedge of cake from the front to form the opening. Cut the un-wedged half in two horizontally and pile up the three pieces of cake, with the wedge piece on top. Layer with butter cream.

3 Add butter cream to the inside of the wedge, then spread a thin layer all over the top and sides. Chill to firm.

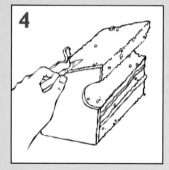

Roll out the brown icing and cut pieces to cover both ends of the chest, trimming off any excess with a small knife.

5

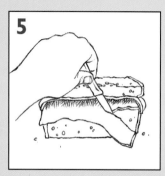

Cover the hollow and the bottom half of the front.

6 Lastly cover the top and back in one piece, trimming the edges neatly

7 Score some wood grain marks with the back of a small knife.

8 Roll out the yellow icing for the straps.

9

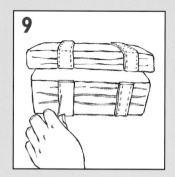

Cut out four long and four short strips 2 cm (¾ in) wide for the straps. Stick to the chest using a little water, trimming as necessary. Mark the detail with a cocktail stick.

10

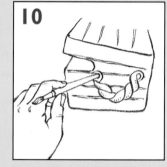

Roll out two thin 20 cm (8 in) long sausages from the yellow trimmings, fold each one in half and twist. Stick in place with a little water, indenting the ends with the handle of a paintbrush.

11 Cut out some yellow icing for the lock and stick on.

12 Use more yellow icing to cover the board. Brush on edible glue and sprinkle on brown sugar for the sand.

13 Stick on the coins, necklaces and sweets with the edible glue.

Pink Princess

A little girl's dream! This cake is made using a real doll — much easier and, I think, much prettier than modelling an icing one or using one of those china 'crinoline lady' cake tops. You can use a favourite doll, or it would be very special to buy a new one and make it an extra present (or buy a doll pick, see page 16). You could, at a push, use a pudding basin instead of the tiffin, but it will make the poor doll look a little dumpy — not a look that any of us would choose.

1 tiffin sponge cake
(see pages 8–9)

1 quantity butter cream
(see page 11)

750 g (1 lb 10 oz) pink roll-out icing

25 silver balls

Pink food colour

Pink iridescent sparkles or edible glitter

1 packet of Barbie glitter gel icing tubes

1 Barbie-style doll, about 28 cm (11 in) high, unclothed

Blossom cutters (see page 15)

25 cm (10 in) round cake board

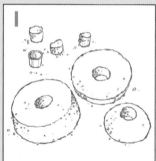

1 Wrap clingfilm around the doll's legs up to her waist and tie her hair back. Cut the cake into three even sections horizontally. With a cutter or sharp knife, cut a hole in the centre of each section large enough for the doll's legs.

2 Sandwich the cake back together with butter cream and stick it to the cake board with a little butter cream. Place the doll in the hole. Spread a thin layer of butter cream all over the cake. Chill to firm.

Using 50 g (1¾ oz) of the pink icing, make eight thin sausages and stick them to the skirt (these will make the folds).

4 Roll out 500 g (1 lb 2 oz) pink icing into an oblong about 50 × 15 cm (20 × 6 in). Roll the icing on to the pin and then unroll it around the cake

making sure that the join is at the back. Trim off the excess down the join, the waist and around the base of the skirt and smooth down the icing with your thumbs to define the folds.

5 Thinly roll out 50 g (1¾ oz) pink icing. Cut out small flowers using the medium-sized blossom cutter and, with a little water, stick a row around her waist, with a silver ball in the centre of each, or use ready-made sugar flowers. Roll out the remaining icing. Paint with pink food colour mixed with a little water and scatter with sparkles.

Cut out two 5 cm (2 in) squares and two 8 × 1.5 cm (3 × ⅝ in) strips. Brush a little water on the doll's body. Place one square on the front of the torso and smooth down the edges. Using a little water, stick the other square on the back and then thin strips around the top. Pipe decoration on to the dress with the glitter gels.

7 Undo the doll's hair and sprinkle with the pink iridescent sparkles.

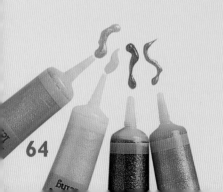

Butterflies & Flowers

The principle of this is very easy and is an effective way of producing a three-dimensional cake without any modelling. The cookies can always be made a few days in advance and kept in an airtight container – I recommend making some extra ones as they're always popular at parties. I've added a few plastic fairies to bring the scene to life – they make great going-home presents if you include one for each guest.

1 quantity vanilla cookie dough – makes about 26 cookies (see page 10)

2 quantities butter cream (see page 11)

Green food colour

25 cm (10 in) square sponge cake (see page 8)

1 quantity royal icing, coating consistency (see page 11)

For decorating
Selection of food colours

Pack of writing icing tubes or gels

Selection of decorations such as gold and silver balls, piped flowers, rainbow strands etc

Pale green iridescent sparkles or edible glitter

Flower and butterfly cookie cutters or templates cut from card

8 wooden kebab sticks

35 cm (14 in) square cake board

1 Preheat the oven to Gas Mark 6/200°C (fan oven 180°C)/400°F and lightly grease two baking trays.

2 Roll out the cookie dough on a lightly floured surface to about 5 mm (¼ in) thick. Cut out seven flowers and five butterfly shapes. Re-roll the trimmings and, with a small sharp knife, cut out some grasses and toadstools.

3 Push the kebab sticks into eight of the butterflies and flowers. Put all the shapes on the baking trays and cook for about 12 minutes, or until golden brown around the edges. Leave on the tray for 5 minutes and then transfer to a cooling rack until cold.

4 Colour the butter cream green. Put the cake on the board and cover the top and sides with the green icing, spiking up the top with a fork to look grassy. Spread a thin layer of butter cream on the board around the cake.

5 Colour the royal icing in batches using different food colours. Decorate the cookies by piping outlines with the writing icing or gel. Colour inside the lines with the royal icing, spreading it with the back of a spoon. Now add decorations to the damp icing. Alternatively, you could just spread the shapes with differently coloured royal icing and add sprinkles and sweets.

6 Arrange the cookies on the cake, sticking the skewered ones into the top first and pressing the others into the icing around the top and sides. Sprinkle with the green sparkles.

Letter Blocks

This is a cute and charming cake (or should I say cakes?) for a young child's birthday party, but it would also be good for christenings or other naming celebrations. It's a bit fiddly covering the cakes with icing, which is why I've kept them quite large, but if you were to make a rich fruit cake and let it mature for a few weeks it would be firm enough to make smaller blocks.

25 cm (10 in) square sponge cake (see pages 8–9)

2 quantities butter cream (see page 11)

750 g (1 lb 10 oz) pale blue roll-out icing

750 g (1 lb 10 oz) pale pink roll-out icing

750 g (1 lb 10 oz) pale yellow roll-out icing

750 g (1 lb 10 oz) pale green roll-out icing

750 g (1 lb 10 oz) pale lilac roll-out icing

Letter and number cookie cutters and mini animal cutters

30 cm (12 in) square cake board

1 Split the cake in half and sandwich together with butter cream.

2 Cut the cake into squares 6 × 6 cm (2½ × 2½ in). Spread each block with a thin layer of butter cream and chill to firm.

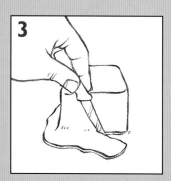

Roll out the pale shades of icing and cover each block separately, by draping the icing over and smoothing gently with your hands. Trim away the excess round the bottom.

Roll out the remaining icing thinly and cut out letter, animal and flower shapes. Stick them to the blocks with a paintbrush dipped in a little water. Stack the cakes up on the board.

An Easy Baby

All together now – Aaaaaaaaaaaaahhhhh...
Isn't he – or she – just cute? This cake would be
wonderful for a tea party to welcome a baby – or for an
informal christening or naming celebration. You can also
see the potential of using this very simple sandwich cake
idea for all kinds of other characters (the Snowman on
pages 20–21, for example). You've only got to add some
cut-out strips of icing 'clothes' to turn it into anything
from Father Christmas to Obi Wan Kenobi.

2 x 18 cm (7 in) round
sandwich sponge cakes
(see pages 8–9)

1 quantity butter cream
(see page 11)

1 kg (2 lb 4 oz) pale pink
roll-out icing

150 g (5½ oz) white roll-
out icing

Pink food colour

25 g (1 oz) black roll-out
icing

40 x 30 cm (16 x 12 in)
cake board

1 Cover the cakes with the butter cream, then cover with two-thirds of the pink icing (see Snowman, page 20, Step 2). Mark the belly button with the end of a paintbrush.

3 Keeping back a little to make the toes, nose and cheeks, divide the remaining pink icing into three. Roll out one piece into a sausage 25 cm (10 in) long. Cut in half and stick to the body for the arms.

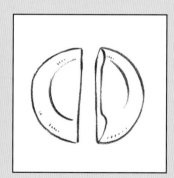

thumb in the middle to about halfway depth, and then cut in half and stick to each side of the head for the ears.

With the kept back pink icing, make five balls of decreasing size for each foot and stick to the feet for toes.

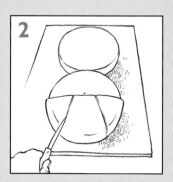

Roll out the white icing as thinly as possible. Cut one end in a straight line, then stick to the cake with a little water to make the nappy. Smooth it around the bottom edge of the cake, trim the edges and mark the nappy lines with the back of a knife.

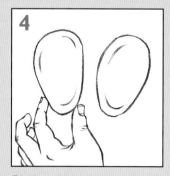

Divide another piece in two and roll into short sausages about 6 cm (2½ in) long. Taper one end of each and flatten to form the feet. Stick on the cake.

5 With the last third of the pink icing, roll a ball about 5 cm (2 in) diameter. Press your

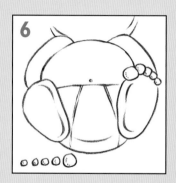

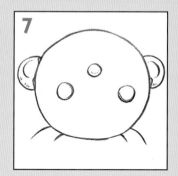

Add a small ball for the nose and two flattened balls for the cheeks, darkening them with a little watered-down pink colouring.

8 Lastly, make two eyes, a big smiley mouth and a tuft of hair out of the black icing and stick on.

Christening Cup Cakes

See how elegant the humble cup cake can be! This is a good example of just how stunning they look when decorated and presented in the right way. This arrangement should look refined rather than raffish, so I suggest sticking to a small palette of colours — allowing the beautiful edible sparkle and delicate decorations to shine out. This idea would be terrific for a wedding cake centrepiece.

1 quantity sponge mix (see page 8)

1 quantity royal icing, coating consistency (see page 11)

Wafer roses, whole crystallised violets, piped flowers and silver balls or heart chocolate dragees

1 pot of white iridescent sparkle or edible glitter

18–20 silver cup cake cases

Bun or muffin tray

Cup cake stand (optional)

I Preheat the oven to Gas Mark 4/180°C (fan oven160°C)/350°F. Put the cup cake cases into a bun or muffin tin and, with a spoon, half-fill the cases with the sponge mix. Bake for about 10–15 minutes until firm to the touch and golden brown. Remove from the tin and allow to cool completely on a rack. If the buns have domed during cooking, trim off the tops so they are level and below the tops of the cases.

Use a teaspoon to spoon icing on to the top of each cake, letting it spread right to the edges of the case.

3 Allow the iced cakes to set slightly before adding the decorations. Finally, sprinkle with a little edible sparkle on top and arrange on a stand (or differently sized cake boards, supported on glasses).

Smartie Wedding

There's something about Smarties that always makes me want to smile – and there aren't many better occasions for smiles than weddings. The shot glasses make fantastic 'pillars' and take the edge off the formality of the tiered arrangement. Once the cake is dismantled and cut, the shot glasses with a bottle of Tequila might come in very handy for the best man and bridesmaids at the evening disco. A single tier makes a good cake for birthdays and Valentine's Day.

15 cm (6 in), 20 cm (8 in) and 25 cm (10 in) round sponge cakes (see pages 8–9)

3 quantities butter cream (see page 11)

2.25 kg (5 lb) white roll-out icing

12 tubes of Smarties for colours shown, 7 for mixed

50 g (1³/₄ oz) red roll-out icing

1 tube of white decorating icing

Red food colour

1 pot of red iridescent sparkles or edible glitter

Some extra red Smarties to fill the shot glasses

Large (2.5 cm) and small (1 cm) heart-shaped cutters

10 x large white hearts on wires (see pages 13 and 17)

10 x small hearts on wires (see pages 13 and 17)

1 posy pick (see page 16)

8 x 20 cm (8 in) plastic cake dowels (see page 16)

8 shot glasses

20 cm (8 in), 25 cm (10 in), 30 cm (12 in) cake boards

1 Split all three sponges in half, and then sandwich them back together with the butter cream.

2 Spread each cake, over the top and sides, with a thin layer of butter cream. Chill in the fridge to firm.

3 Put each cake on to a board, according to its size. Now roll out the white icing. Cover the three cakes and their boards with white icing, using roughly 450 g, 550 g and 750 g respectively. Trim as necessary.

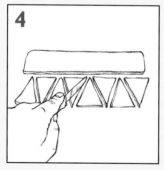

Roll out the icing trimmings and cut out 5–7 triangles about 5 cm (2 in) long.

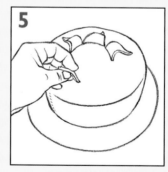

Stick them to the top tier with a little water for the 'explosion'.

6 Stick a row of Smarties around the top and bottom edges of each cake with white decorating icing.

7 Roll out the red icing and cut out red hearts. Stick

them to the sides of the cake with a little water.

8 Paint five of the small and five of the large wired hearts with red food colour, then dip them into red glitter. Leave to dry.

9 Insert the posy pick in the centre of the 'explosion' and add the wired hearts. Fill in any gaps with white icing to hold firm.

10 Add five dowels to the bottom cake and three to the middle one (see page 13).

11 Fill the shot glasses with the extra Smarties. Sit each glass on the dowels and set the cakes on the glasses.

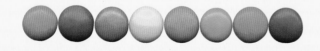

Love Heart Wedding

These romantic sweets were around when I was a teenager, and it's delightful that they've re-emerged as a favourite today. Used on a cake like this, they avoid over-formality and fussiness, without entirely destroying the theme of the occasion which is, of course, love, love and yet more love. Don't be put off by the list of bits and pieces – you can quite well do without the cutter and piping bag if you like, simply add some extra, smaller sweets as decoration.

15 cm (6 in), 20 cm (8 in) and 25 cm (10 in) round sponge cakes (see pages 8–9)

3 quantities butter cream (see page 11)

1 kg (2 lb 4 oz) pink roll-out icing

750 g (1 lb 10 oz) white roll-out icing

1 quantity royal icing (see page 11)

3 packets Love Heart sweets

Silver balls

6 x 20 cm (8 in) plastic cake dowels (see page 16)

Large blossom plunger cutter

Piping bag with adaptor and no. 3 nozzle

15 cm (6 in) and 20 cm (8 in) round thin cake boards

30 cm (12 in) round thick cake board

1 Split all three cakes in two horizontally and sandwich together with butter cream. Spread a thin layer of butter cream over the top and sides of each and chill to firm. Place the 25 cm (10 in) round cake on the 30 cm (12 in) thick cake board and cover the cake with 750 g (1 lb 10 oz) pink icing. Trim the bottom edge neatly.

2 Put the 20 cm (8 in) cake on its thin board. Add 500 g (1 lb 2 oz) of white icing to the remaining pink and knead together. Roll out 500 g of it and cover the 20 cm (8 in) cake.

3 Add three dowels to the 25 cm (10 in) cake, as shown on page 13. Spread a little royal icing over the top.

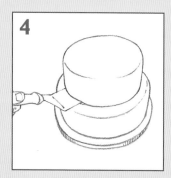

Put the 20 cm (8 in) cake with its board on top of the 25 cm (10 in) cake, making sure that it is centred.

5 Put the 15 cm (6 in) cake on to its thin board. Add 200 g (7 oz) white icing to the

remaining pale pink icing, knead well, roll out and cover cake.

6 Add three dowels to the 20 cm (8 in) cake. Spread the top of the cake with a little royal icing. Add the 15 cm (6 in) cake, making sure it is centred.

With no. 3 nozzle in place, fill the piping bag with royal icing and pipe small dots around the base of each tier.

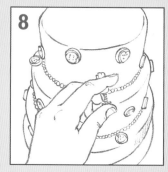

Stick on Love Heart sweets with royal icing around all three tiers and add a small pile to the top of the cake.

9 Thinly roll out the remaining 50 g white roll-out icing and cut out blossom flowers. Stick on to the cake with a little water. Pipe a small dot of royal icing into the centres of the flowers and stick on silver balls to finish.

Chocolate Wedding

Many young couples choose to have sponge cakes for their weddings nowadays, whether chocolate or plain, and there are all kinds of ways to make them look celebratory. On this cake the contrast of white and chocolate Maltesers looks surprisingly classy. One layer would make a great cake for a special tea.

- 15 cm (6 in) and 25 cm (10 in) round chocolate sponge cakes (see pages 8–9)
- 2 quantities butter cream (see page 11)
- 2 quantities chocolate fudge icing (see page 10)
- Approx 70 milk chocolate Maltesers or 4 x 37 g packets
- Approx 82 white Maltesers or 5 x 35 g packets
- 10 physalis (Cape gooseberries), 1 sheet gold leaf and 8 cm (3 in) circle of card (optional)
- 3 x 20 cm (8 in) plastic cake dowels (see page 16)
- 30 cm (12 in) round cake board
- 15 cm (6 in) round thin cake board

1 Split each of the sponges in half and fill with butter cream. Spread the top and sides of both, thinly, with more butter cream.

2 Put the 25 cm (10 in) cake on the 30 cm (12 in) round cake board and the small cake on the 15 cm (6 in) round thin board. Place both in the fridge for about 30 minutes to firm up.

3 Spread the fudge icing over the top and sides of both the cakes with a palette knife. Either mark the top and sides with the flat of a knife as I've done, or leave the surface rough.

4 Add the three dowels to the large cake as shown on page 13.

5 Place the small cake on top of the larger cake and arrange the Maltesers around the base of each tier and on the top.

6 Gild the physalis with the gold leaf, using a dry brush. Stick five to a small circle of card using a little butter cream and put on the centre top. Arrange the rest on the lower tier.

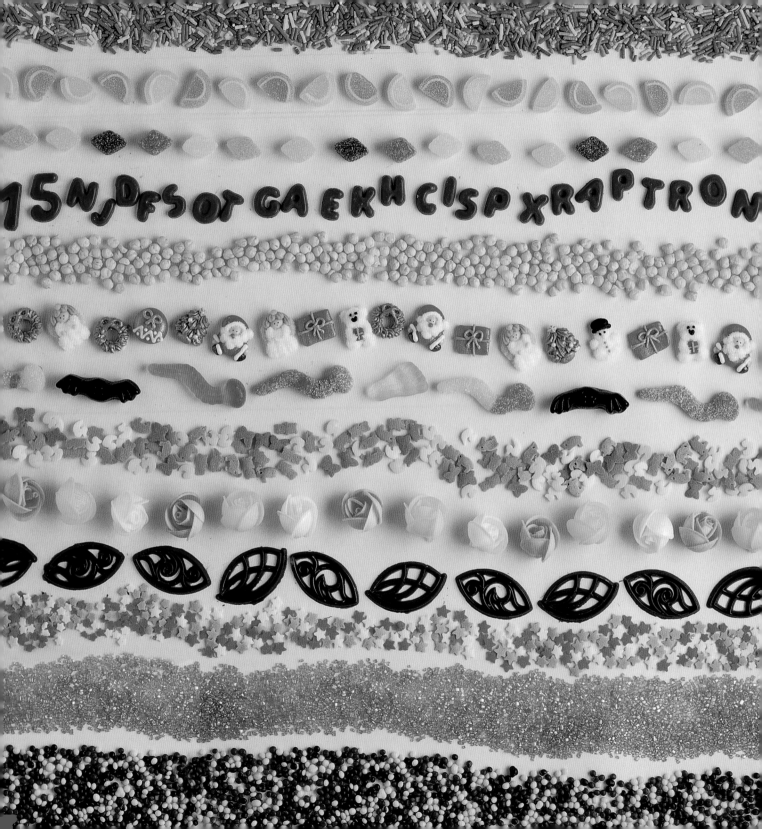